Drawing Is Basic
Drawing and Writing to Learn

GRADE 4

Drawing is a basic way of seeing and expressing. Every child can draw, but too many children are daunted by the fear that what they draw will not look "right." It is your joyous opportunity to encourage each of your students to draw and write with comfort and confidence.

Jean Morman Unsworth

DALE SEYMOUR PUBLICATIONS®

Parsippany, New Jersey

Editorial Manager: Carolyn Coyle
Senior Editor: Mary Ellen Gilbert
Production/Manufacturing Director: Janet Yearian
Production/Manufacturing Manager: Karen Edmonds
Production/Manufacturing Coordinator: Lorraine Allen
Art Director: Jim O'Shea
Text and Cover Design: Robert Dobaczewski

Credits

Corot, Jean-Baptiste Camille, *Souvenir D'Ostie,* p. 30. From the collection of Jean and Tim Unsworth.

Corinth, Lovis, 1858–1925, *Homework,* p. 60. 1916, lithograph; *Reiterferd (Horse and Rider),* p. 69, 1916, lithograph. Courtesy of R. S. Johnson International Gallery, Chicago, IL.

Rebora, Joyce Kuhlmann, *Ears of Corn,* p. 35, pen and ink. Courtesy of the artist.

Unsworth, Jean Morman, *Tree Branches, Point Lobos, California,* p. 31, pencil; *Milkweed Pods,* p. 32, ink and wash; *Pine Cone,* p. 32, pencil; *Group of Students,* p. 61, marker; *Egyptian Tomb Relief,* p. 65, photograph; *Animal in Motion,* p. 67, pencil; *Egret,* p. 70, pen and ink; *Mt. Vernon, George Washington's Home,* p. 77, photograph; *Tellaro, Italy,* p. 79, pencil; *St. Cirq Lapopie, Dordogne, France,* p. 80, pen and ink; *Badlands, South Dakota,* p. 82, pencil.

Dale Seymour Publications
An imprint of Pearson Learning
299 Jefferson Road, P.O. Box 480
Parsippany, New Jersey 07054-0480

www.pearsonlearning.com

1-800-321-3106

Dale Seymour Publications® is a registered trademark of Dale Seymour Publications, Inc.

ISBN 0-7690-2500-5

1 2 3 4 5 6 7 8 9 10-ML-04 03 02 01 00

This Book Is Printed
On Recycled Paper

This book is dedicated to children of all ages who have and who will discover that their eyes are their keys to drawing. I wish them the joy of seeing and the pleasure of recording the things they see and the ideas they imagine. I wish them the confidence in drawing that is their birthright.

Jean Morman Unsworth

Thanks to the teachers who piloted the lessons in *Drawing Is Basic* and who sent in their students' drawings.

Lin Ferrell
Visual Arts Instructional Specialist
Chesterfield County Public Schools
Richmond, Virginia, and the
art teachers of Chesterfield County

Teri Power, art specialist
School District of
New Richmond, Wisconsin

Eva Dubowski, art teacher
Infant of Prague School
Flossmoor, Illinois

Andrea Rowe, classroom teacher
St. Damian School
Oak Forest, Illinois

Catherine Kestler, art teacher,
and classroom teachers of
Sacred Heart Academy
Chicago, Illinois

Barbara Perez, art teacher
St. Athanasius School
Evanston, Illinois

Dorothy Johnson, art supervisor
Volusia County Schools
Florida

Wanda Baer, art teacher
Mount Carmel Academy
Chicago, Illinois

Additional thanks to the classroom teachers in the following Chicago, Illinois, schools: St. Matthias School, Children of Peace School, and St. Gertrude School.

A special thank you to all the young artists who performed the drawing exercises in this book and whose drawings add a unique charm to *Drawing Is Basic*.

Peter Johnson	Jennifer Anagnost	Moira O'Neil
Tom Curran	Albert Starshak	Jason DeHaan
Tim Curran	Richard Ignacz	Steven Atkinson
Jolie Dubowski	Ashley Dinzey	Katrina Speck
Vincent Ferrari	Cristina Viars	Marcus Brown
Peter Staub	Elizabeth Ospina	Erica Claire Hatten
Kimeyo Rogers	Melissa Radke	Christopher Eric Norwood
Julian Longino	Ray O'Connell	Josh Mullen
Briana Hargraves	Hanna Folz	Krissy Etz
Jessica Krumb	Vince Carioscia	Dipali Patel
Bill Dominic Mammosen	Jill Mettler	Nicole Justice
E. J. McNeil	Alex Olson	Joey Stemmle
Erin Fenn	Jessica Abramson	Srikar Bongu
Sara Kors	Shane Martin	Travanti Rader
Stacie Downs	Laura Buttitta	Taneisha Rachal
Mollie Headley	Alex Seratoni	Sarah O'Malley
Sarah Engelbach	Caitlyn Baker	Jack Hauck
Sheila McCarroll	Kevin McCarthy	Barry Jackson
Maddie Flanagan	Zachary Parkes	Sean Bowen
Crissy Johnson	Danh Tran	Monica Kusaka
Joyce Poe	Anna Teske	James Meuhleman
Dominic Fosco	Alexandra Gecker	Colin Ryan
Blayke Anderson	Billy Figueroa	Stella Ryan-Lozon
Ashley Bush	Vernes Seferovic	Maria Troy
Dominic Ruffin	Abby Gravenhorst	Kimberly Hudson
Bruce Baskerville	Dan Rowe	Nhat Tran
Meredith Steinhauser	Mimi Nguyen	Wesley Wright
Tom Robbins	Beth Faydel	Luis Estrada
Nicole Figueroa	John Wojcik	Mari Kiedysz
Samantha McCarthy	Patrick Kasten	Derek Wells

Contents

1. Daily Exercises
   in Perception

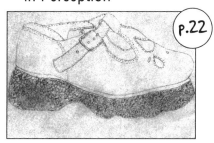

p.22

2. Connecting to All of
   Your Senses

p.25

3. Drawing Flowers

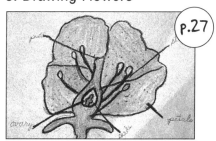

p.27

4. Drawing Trees

p.29

5. Drawing Textures

p.32

6. Drawing Food

p.34

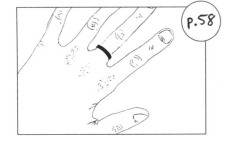

22. Cutting Figures

p.63

23. Animating Cut Figures

p.64

24. Finding Subjects in Your Studies

p.65

25. Drawing Animals

p.67

26. Drawing Birds

p.70

27. Drawing Fish and Other Sea Creatures

p.72

28. Drawing Insects

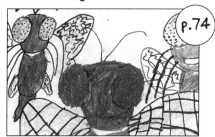

p.74

29. Drawing Architecture

p.76

30. Drawing Your Travels— Real or Wished For

p.80

31. Drawing Maps

p.83

32. Drawing from Imagination

p.86

33. Encouraging Drawing at Home

p.89

A Message to the Classroom Teacher

IT IS WITHIN THE POWER OF EVERY PERSON TO DRAW.

The natural condition of the human organism is joy. Ecstasy is not opposed to reason and order. Much of the life of the child is learning, making connections. It is momentous, joyous. It must not be quelled.

—George Leonard, *Education and Ecstasy*

Drawing is an essential means of expression, just as important as written and oral expression in the daily work of learning. Drawing is a complementary mode of learning. It helps complete written and verbal communication. Visual thinking is a dynamic element of learning. As a classroom teacher, you can teach visual thinking through drawing. It is important that you never draw for children, but that you motivate them to look and to draw with their eyes. You can help them to see details and understand proportions, but the drawing is theirs.

Here are some important points to keep in mind about drawing.

❖ Drawing is as personal as handwriting. We all learn to shape cursive letters the same way. Yet we each develop a unique style of handwriting that is our identification. Our drawing styles must be equally personal. Don't attempt to teach a student what something should look like; rather, teach how to look. Students will see uniquely, according to their level of maturity and keenness of perception.

❖ When you teach perception, you are at the same time teaching reading. Reading begins with following a line of letters and looking carefully. **Perceptual** drawing helps develop that skill in a child.

❖ When students (or adults) draw by letting their eyes direct their hands, their concentration is beautiful. Try taking a drawing/writing break when your students are restless. It calms and centers them. Drawing is like meditation. Set the stage with quiet looking. When students start drawing "with their eyes," they will be very still and focused. They will go back to their other lessons relaxed and ready.

❖ Yes, there are artistically talented students, just as there are talented dancers, mathematicians, scientists, and so on. We would never accept the excuse, "I don't write beautifully, so I won't write." So, too, "I don't draw beautifully" is no excuse for not drawing. Third grade is a determining time for all natural-born artists who have drawn happily through their scribbling days—and this is just about every child. Too often, children at this age begin to judge their drawings and decide that they "can't draw." Unfortunately, this fallacy continues throughout their lives. I have seen very bright children who will not draw. They have been so conditioned to getting the "right answer" that they find risking an "unsuccessful" drawing to be traumatic. Encouraging students to take risks is the most important lesson you can teach them. It will affect all of their learning.

❖ My experience with teachers as well as students has proven to me that it is linear thinking that stifles individuals' drawing. Once empowered to risk drawing with their eyes—in other words, really following edges with their eyes and letting their hands record them—everyone can draw. Try drawing your own shoe (see the directions on page 22) and trusting your eyes. More classroom teachers than I can count have done this exercise in my workshops and were so astounded at their drawings that they wanted to take them home and frame them. Often, these same teachers, who formerly believed they could not draw, would never have initiated an art lesson in their classrooms.

❖ Drawing should be a means of expressing learning in every subject. The arts are unique in their potential to develop a healthy and productive attitude toward risk-taking and learning from failure. Often the failure of creative ideas stimulates new and better ideas.

❖ Howard Gardner's theory of multiple intelligences has extended our understanding of how we learn. Linguistic intelligence and logical-mathematical intelligence are only two of the ways that we can learn. Spatial intelligence, or the ability to perceive form and give visual shape to ideas, is of equal importance to many students. Some students respond much more readily to visual learning than to linear logic. The right-brain-dominant child will  often resist a linear approach. Also, students whose family experiences have not encouraged reading and factual mastery will often be unprepared for the regimen of school, but will draw happily and readily.

❖ Training students' eyes to really see is our first task as teachers. You, as a classroom teacher, should be a part of this visual learning. In an interdisciplinary learning climate, every subject should be approached both literally and expressively. A once-a-week art lesson by an art specialist cannot begin to reach these dimensions. When you help your students to develop basic drawing skills, you will enable the art specialist to move in leaps rather than slow steps.

Goals of Teaching Drawing

The real point about art education is that we must create whole human beings, people who are alive to their fingertips; people who are in a responsible attitude to sensation, to every organized form, to every meaning of the world about them. To open the closed eye is the first lesson of art in our time; the second is to open the inner eye, the eye of vision and dream.

—Lewis Mumford

❖ To develop in all students the skill and confidence to draw with their eyes so that they will be able to use drawing as a complementary and essential mode of learning in all subjects.

❖ To stimulate visual perception in every child.

❖ To teach students the language of art—how to look for lines, shapes, spaces, textures, and colors all around them.

❖ To make students aware of the principles of art—rhythm, balance, proportion—as they occur in movement and sound as well as in visual form.

❖ To nurture students' sensory perception through all their senses. Have them spend time touching, looking, listening, smelling, tasting, and describing their perceptions.

❖ To spur your students' imaginations, encourage them to risk trying new ideas and to help them create, invent, connect, experiment with, and enjoy their own ideas.

❖ To nurture in all students the ability to express both their drawing and their seeing in words. Each daily fifteen-minute drawing/writing period should include five minutes to write about what they have drawn or about the experience of drawing. Encourage students to keep a journal in which they write briefly about things they see.

❖ To allow yourself the joy of drawing, thus building your own confidence and your own vision.

Challenges You May Encounter

Most students at this age love to draw and draw fearlessly, but you may encounter some of the following problems.

❖ **What about the student who will not draw certain kinds of images, such as figures?**
One girl I met said she did not draw figures; she drew trees. She would not even try to draw a figure. This is an example of the fear of risk-taking that students who succeed in "right answer" kinds of testing often experience. By drawing trees, she could meet her expectations for success. The most important lesson that such students need to learn is that taking risks and having failed attempts will enable them to discover new and better ways to succeed.

❖ **What about the student who draws fast and carelessly?**
Use the drawing/writing time to walk around and spot students who need guidance. Quiet concentration and observation need to be cultivated in today's fast-paced world and climate of passive entertainment. "Doing it yourself" needs nurturing in many students. Set the tone before giving the assignment. Prepare sketchbooks or other materials and tools. Model looking carefully at the object to be drawn. Encourage crawling along every edge as if your eye is a bug.

❖ **What about the student who does not seem to see details?**
This may be a sign of a perceptual handicap such as dyslexia or other dysfunctions related to the eye or hand. Spend time with this student. Run your finger along the edge to be drawn. Then have the student do it. Much directed practice will be needed. The better this student can discipline his or her eyes to follow an edge, the better he or she will read.

Drawing Is Basic

Drawing Is Basic is designed for daily fifteen-minute drawing/writing breaks carried out by the classroom teacher as a supplement to a full art curriculum. It is not an art curriculum. As a drill in perception, this program's goal is to make students comfortable with drawing objects and figures. Your students will be able to use this skill in all their subjects. The content of the drawing exercises provided here connects to all curriculum subjects.

Set a time for drawing/writing. An effective plan is to set a time during your day when students typically need a break. Try to plan fifteen minutes each day. You will find that when students draw, they become intensely quiet and involved. It frees them from the response mode and allows them to express themselves. Many times, the drawing/writing break can be a part of a math, social studies, language arts, or science lesson.

With each drawing experience, a corresponding writing exercise is suggested. You may use other writing themes as well. Adapt and modify these drawing and writing ideas in whatever way they best fit your teaching and complement your curriculum.

Keep a journal. Encourage students to keep notebooks of their own in which they can sketch and write observations and ideas each day. Occasionally, take a few minutes to ask them to share an observation from their journals.

Plan. Work on one set of lessons for one to two weeks, depending on the number of lessons you choose to do. Some of the lessons will take longer than the fifteen-minute period. You might carry one through a week, working on it each day. During the first two weeks, you might concentrate on the perceptual drawing lessons—drawing shoes, toys, and so on—and the sensory exercises. Continue these periodically through the school year.

Figure drawing will take many practice sessions. Have students do gesture drawings first, then contour drawings. Follow the sequence of lessons on drawing parts you can't see, drawing action, drawing groups, and so on. Do gesture drawing exercises frequently. When students are secure in posing and drawing figures, they can use these skills to illustrate concepts in other subject matters.

Using the I Am an Artist Sketchbook

The student sketchbooks have a dual purpose.

1. The sketchbooks provide drawing paper for most of your lessons. However, you may want to have students draw on practice paper a few times before using the sketchbooks in some lessons. For cutting lessons, you will want to provide other paper such as construction paper.

2. The sketchbooks also will help you keep a record of students' development. Date pages as students complete them. Periodically use the critiquing techniques beginning on page 18 to help students self-assess their work. Encourage students to keep sketchbooks through the years to see their growth.

Preparing Sketchbook Covers. The sketchbook covers are designed for students' self-portraits. Students can draw their self-portraits in the space provided on the cover, or use other creative ways to make this space their own.

Preparing for the Lessons

The greater the awareness of all the senses, the greater will be the opportunity for learning.

—Viktor Lowenfeld and Lambert W. Brittain

❖ Direct students to take out their sketchbooks or distribute other paper. Select the drawing tool you want students to use or allow them to choose their own.

❖ Introduce the lesson briefly. Then have students begin drawing. Observe students who are having trouble and help them to look carefully at their subjects. Do not draw for them.

❖ Direct students to let their eyes crawl like a bug along each edge, moving from one edge to another. Direct them to let their hands follow the path of their eyes, noting every line and detail.

I have not yet exhausted the ground under my feet.

—Andrew Wyeth

❖ Tell students that they may look at their paper whenever they need to, but they should not draw again until their eyes are on the objects. They may extend lines to close a shape in their drawings, but they should look back at their subjects before continuing to draw.

❖ Encourage drawing a flowing line rather than several sketchy lines. The eye and hand will not work together if one is moving along and the other is not.

❖ Don't be satisfied with tiny little drawings or drawings done without looking. A quick circle for an apple is not a perceptual drawing. Take time to hold an apple up and ask for descriptions of its shape.

❖ At the end of each lesson, allow four or five minutes for students to write a sentence or two about their drawing experience or about the subjects of their drawings. Share these writings periodically by having students read them aloud.

Tools and Materials

Drawing Tools

Each drawing tool has its own potential and characteristics. This drawing program focuses on the basic tools, but even these offer a wide range of possibilities of **line quality** and texture. Vary the tools your students use in the daily exercises. Encourage them to experiment with each tool.

Drawing with pencil. For best results, use an ebony pencil for drawing. It has dark, soft lead, and can make a whole range of tones from black to gray. Experiment by pressing heavily and lightly. Show students how to hold it on its side to make thick and thin lines.

Drawing with crayon. Encourage students to try pressing heavily or lightly as they draw with crayons. You might have them create watercolor resists over hard waxy lines and shapes.

Drawing with marker. Markers are wonderful for quick sketches. They are also great for doing sensitive lines.

Drawing with charcoal. Charcoal pencils or sticks of charcoal offer a different medium, one that can be blended and smudged for interesting effects. Offer charcoal as an alternative drawing tool.

Experimenting with tools. Use a drawing break to just experiment with each tool. Ask students to draw lines that are

Ask students to think of adjectives and draw lines that look like what the words sound like or mean.

Drawing Materials

Materials for drawing include paper of different sizes and weights. The student sketchbooks will provide drawing paper for most lessons; however, provide students with other paper for practice. Some lessons call for larger sheets of paper, 12" × 18" or 18" × 24". Kraft/mural paper is a good, economical choice. Use mural paper and overhead projectors to enlarge shapes and figures for murals.

For cutting activities, construction paper, scissors, and glue will be needed. For **crayon resist**, paintbrushes, watercolors, and plastic cups of water will be needed.

Classroom Resources

A classroom that is visually exciting is a stimulus to looking, learning, and expressing. There are numerous resources, both for purchase and for free, that can add visual energy to your classroom. Display various objects in your classroom and encourage students to pick them up, examine them, and feel them. Here are some ideas for creating a climate that stimulates visual learning in your classroom.

❖ A place for found objects—such as stones, small branches, a wheel from a broken toy, and the many other things that students like to collect—is a source of ideas for drawing. Place the objects in a box or on a small table.

❖ Make nature photographs, videos, and math manipulatives available to students. Tapes of educational television programs can be rich resources. Pause videos to allow students to look carefully at birds, animals, flowers, and so on. Study shapes, colors, and the patterns on fish, zebras, and other forms.

❖ Ask students to bring in their favorite toys. Encourage students to look at, feel, and notice the details of many different objects.

❖ Create a texture board or box. Encourage students to bring in pieces of cloth, paper, or other things with textured surfaces. Develop their vocabularies by describing the textures.

❖ Check out birds, boxes of butterflies, and other natural objects from your local nature museum.

❖ Visit zoos, museums, and other exhibits with students to stimulate interest in recording what they see. Encourage students to use their sketchbooks on these visits.

❖ Encourage students to take their sketchbooks and journals on family trips and draw what they see.

❖ Invite students to bring family ethnic costumes or memorabilia to class. Have students pose wearing their costumes or have them hold their special objects while other students draw.

Critiquing Techniques

Do each of the exercises several times with students. Each experience of intent looking will sharpen students' perception and improve their drawing. Periodically allow time for your students to review their drawings and critique their own progress. Encourage honest criticism, both positive and negative.

It is important to establish a climate for positive criticism in your classroom. Here are some ideas to accomplish this. You might say:

❖ This drawing exercise is eye training, not just sketching. We are training our eyes to look more carefully and our hands to work with our eyes.

❖ If you risk not getting it right, your drawing skills will get better and better. If you don't try, your skills won't improve.

❖ Critiquing our work means looking at it to see if it could be better. It is the best way to improve our skills.

❖ We are helping each other when we offer criticism. We are helping ourselves when we decide what could be better in our drawings.

❖ Remember, your drawing is just as much your own as your handwriting. Don't try to copy someone else's drawing. Be confident of your own talents and abilities.

❖ As your sketchbook fills up, go back and compare your early drawings with your new ones to see the improvement.

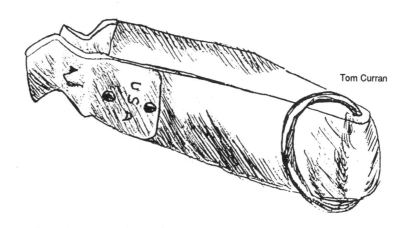

Tom Curran

The Elements of Art

The elements of art—line, shape, texture, color, and space—are like parts of speech in language. They are what you use as you draw, and each element has expressive power. Ask students to look for the following elements of art in their drawings.

Line. Have students talk about lines in their drawings. Ask them if their lines are thick, thin, flowing, or angular. Talk about how drawing tools affect lines.

Shape. Direct students to look at the shape of the objects they drew. Do their drawings look like the objects? Ask them to explain how they drew the shape of the object. Did they change the shape to show something unique about how they saw the object?

Texture. Did students find a way to show how the object they drew feels? Describe textures such as soft, hard, fuzzy, or hairy. How did students show the texture of the object?

Color. If students used color, ask how it added to their drawings. Suggest that if they want to draw a red apple, they use a red crayon to draw its shape as well as its color.

Space. If students' drawings show space in a room or a landscape, ask how they showed it. Did they draw things smaller in the distance? Did they draw objects behind other objects by showing only the parts they could see? Teach foreground, middle ground, and background.

The Principles of Art

The principles of art are the "rules" for organizing elements in artworks. Present the following principles of art to students.

Rhythm. Ask your students to tap out rhythms on their desks such as A, BB, A, BB. Rhythm is a pattern that comes from repetition. Point out to students repeat rows of design, repeat colors, and so on. Help them recognize other examples of visual rhythm.

Balance and Proportion. These principles of art create a pleasing order of size and arrangement of forms in a composition. Teach **bilateral** and **radial symmetry.**

Variety. Teach students to recognize and appreciate the differences, or variety, in shapes, colors, textures, lines, and so on.

Unity. Help students understand the concept of a harmonious composition; a drawing in which all the principles of art work together.

Assessment

This program is designed as a drill in perception, not as a subject to be graded. Make assessment a positive experience. Encourage students to assess their own progress by asking them to compare recent drawings with those completed earlier, and to find ways in which they are improving. Keep and date drawings, especially those in the student sketchbooks, as a means of both teacher and individual assessment. To keep track of students' monthly progress during the school year, duplicate the chart on page 95 for each student. A sample is shown below.

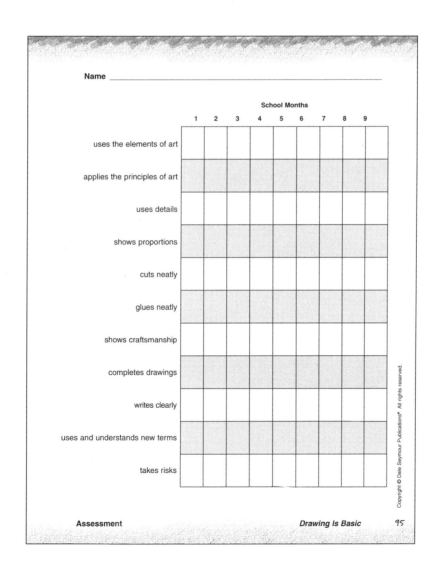

Name _____

School Months

	1	2	3	4	5	6	7	8	9
uses the elements of art									
applies the principles of art									
uses details									
shows proportions									
cuts neatly									
glues neatly									
shows craftsmanship									
completes drawings									
writes clearly									
uses and understands new terms									
takes risks									

Assessment　　　　　　　　　　　　　　　*Drawing Is Basic*　　95

Drawing Exercises

All of the following drawing exercises are written as you would present them to your students. Directions and suggestions for you, the teacher, are in italic type. The ✏ icon indicates teacher dialogue.

1. Daily Exercises in Perception

Create a climate in which students look thoughtfully before they begin drawing. Have them draw on practice paper a few times before drawing in their sketchbooks. Save all drawings so students can compare and critique their own work. Look for that uniqueness and applaud it in each student's work.

Tools: pencils (no erasers), crayons, or markers

✏ *(Explain to the students that they will be doing **contour drawing**—finding all the edges.)* Take off one shoe. Before drawing, take time to turn your shoe around to see that it looks different from each angle. Run your finger along your shoe's lines and decorative details. Place your shoe on your desk. Start drawing the top back of your shoe. Let your eyes move along the edge toward the front. Draw as large as you can. As your eyes move along, let your hand and tool follow the movement. Draw a flowing line. When you need to extend a line to meet and close a shape, look back at your drawing but stop drawing when you do. Do not begin to draw again until your eyes are where you left off on your shoe. Draw every detail you see—lines for the sole, the laces, and so on. These drawings are by fourth graders. Note the three different views—side, top, and back.

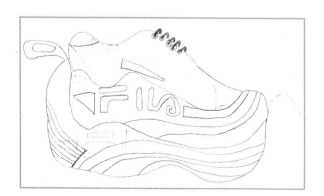

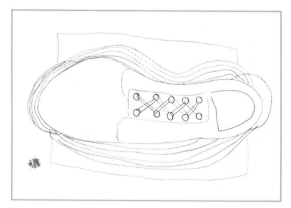

When you have finished drawing, turn your shoe in a different position and draw another view of it. Then draw different views of many kinds of shoes. Choose a drawing tool that will work well for each shoe. Write a story about where your shoes will take you.

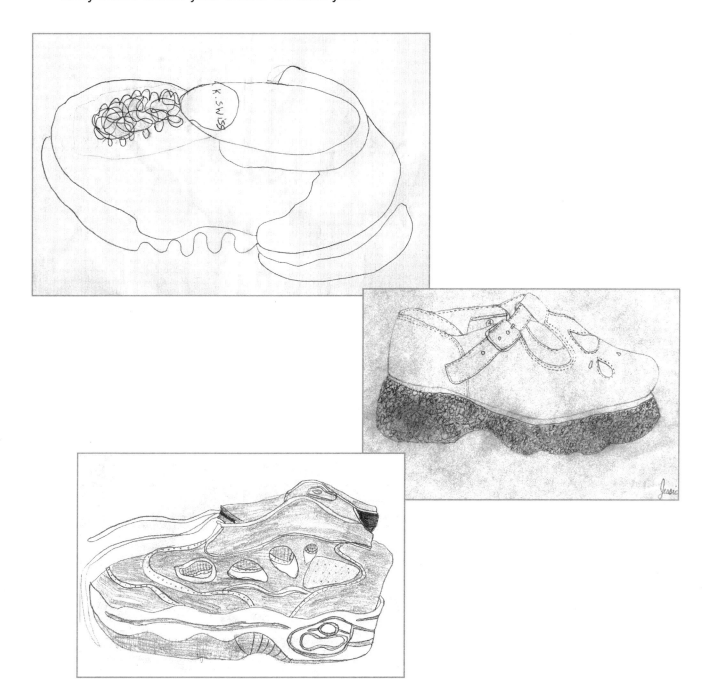

✏ Take out five crayons or markers and lay them on your desk in a row or at an angle. Draw your arrangement. Is it a log jam on a river? Write about what it could be.

✐ Bring in a toy with wheels and draw it. Write about your toy. How does it move?

✐ Draw the clock in your classroom or your wristwatch. Look for every detail. Write about what you could do in an hour.

✐ *(Write spelling words on cards. Give one to each student.)* Draw a picture of your word on a separate piece of paper. Show your drawing to the class. See who can guess the word and spell it correctly.

✐ Draw a pair of scissors closed and then open. List the many uses of scissors.

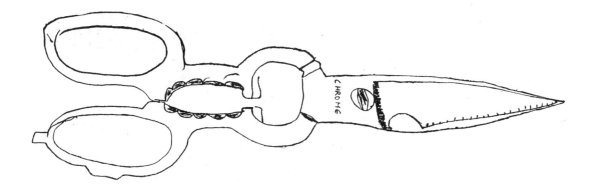

2. Connecting to All of Your Senses

✎ Draw a page of lines and connect adjectives with each one—squiggly, harsh, nervous, quiet, angry, calm, lazy, energetic, and so on. *(Suggest that students keep three drawing tools on their desks and then, for each adjective, choose the one that will work best.)*

To prepare for the exercise that follows, put small objects such as empty toothpaste tubes, seashells, golf balls, kernels of popcorn, and bottle caps in brown paper lunch bags. Distribute one bag to each student.

✎ Do not look in the bag. Use your sense of touch. Feel an object in the bag with one hand as you draw with the other. Feel all the edges and draw what they feel like. Don't just identify your object. Write about it when you have finished.

Arrange students in pairs. Blindfold one and have the other lead his or her partner around the room to touch, describe, and identify objects. Change roles after a few minutes.

✐ Take a blind walk. Write about the experience.

✐ *(Give a small shell or pretzel to each student.)* Use your memory. Look carefully at your shell (or pretzel) for a full minute. Now put it away and draw all the details you remember. When you have finished, write about what you have learned.

✐ *(Distribute a saltine cracker to each student.)* Use all of your senses. Feel the cracker. Look at it and smell it. Write five adjectives that describe it. Break the cracker and eat it. Write two more adjectives about it. Now use your memory to draw the cracker as large as you can in your sketchbook. Be sure to add all the details, including the salt crystals.

3. Drawing Flowers

Distribute real or artificial flowers to each student. Teach the parts of a flower so students will find and draw the pistil, stamen, petals, sepal, stem, roots, and leaves.

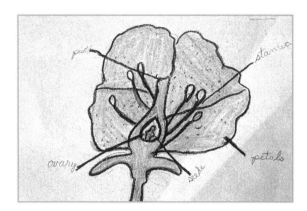

- Some flowers are bilaterally symmetrical—the same on both sides. Find flowers or leaves that are bilaterally symmetrical and draw them. Design some flowers of your own. Write a poem about a flower.

- Draw a flower, and label all its parts. Try to draw the petals so they look soft. Note the shape of the leaves and the bend of the stem. Describe the flower.

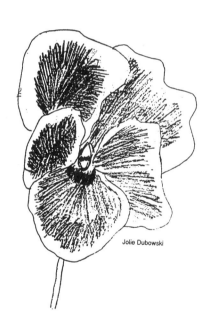

Jolie Dubowski

- Draw a flower garden as a bee would see it—from above. Fill your paper with many colors and shapes of flowers. Write a bee's reaction to it.

You might ask students to do the following experiment at home over a period of a few weeks. Have them plant an onion and draw several stages of the onion's growth. If you conduct the experiment in the classroom, place the onion plant in the center of the room. Ask students to turn their desks toward it so each student will have a different view. Compare views when the students have finished.

- Plant an onion in a glass of water, using toothpicks to support the onion on the edge of the glass. Keep the glass full of water. Watch the roots develop and draw a sequence of growth sketches. Keep a diary of the onion's progress.

This drawing of a tree's flowering branch was done with a fine-point marker. Find examples of trees that flower such as magnolia, lilac, apple, and cherry. Draw the tree's flowering branch. Write a poem using five participles describing your branch. This is one student's poem.

Flipping, flopping,

curving, stopping,

always dancing with the wind.

Draw a plant. Look for all the branches and leaves on it. This is a student's drawing.

28

4. Drawing Trees

The growth pattern called organic branching is found in many forms in nature. Start with a bulletin board of branching forms. Ask your students to bring in pictures or diagrams of everything from a small twig to a photo of human blood vessels. Lightning branches; cracks in the sidewalk branch; rivers branch. Connect this to geography. Each species of tree has a unique branching pattern. Send students to the library, the Internet, books, and magazines to find and gather pictures of many species of trees.

Take students outside on a nice day with pencils and sketchbooks. Find a tree and tell your students to start at the base and "climb up the trunk with their eyes."

✐ Pretend your eye is a bug crawling up the tree. Follow the line out to a branch. See it connect to a smaller branch. Bring the line back, giving the branch thickness. Keep your eyes on the tree. Note the lines of branches going behind other branches. The foliage can be drawn any way you see it. Look at these drawings and the different ways foliage was drawn. These pictures show that the students were really looking.

A Weeping Maple Tree is as tall as a strong, young basketball star.

Maria T.

The Weeping Maple ...nds like it's waiting ... someone to cheer ...em up.

Kimberly Hudson   Weeping Maple

✐ Do rubbings of several leaves. Use different colors of crayon and create a pleasing composition on your paper. See page 41 for lessons about composition.

✏ Write a poem or a haiku about a tree. A haiku is a Japanese poetry form that has seventeen syllables—five in the first line, seven in the second, and five in the third. This is a student's haiku.

Up to the blue sky

Golden Maple's branches reach

High above the rest.

✏ Choose a tree and practice different ways of drawing foliage. You might draw each leaf, scribble clusters of leaves, or build up many tiny lines to make a large mass. Study the way French artist Camille Corot (KOR-O) built up the shape of trees—their trunks, branches. and leaves—with many fine lines. Write a simile about your tree such as "tall as a skyscraper," or write a metaphor, such as "the maple tree in its dark leaf-green uniform."

✏ Collect some leaves of different sizes and shapes. Turn up the veined underside of a leaf and do a rubbing. Place a sheet of paper over the leaf and rub it with the side of a crayon. Write about two other things that have veins.

✏ Start with a line drawn in the center of your paper. Then draw lines on each side, making them branch as they go up. Think of the rings of a tree's growth. Build up a trunk and branches. Write about how long a tree lives. Think about the giant Sequoias in the western part of the United States. These are two examples. Each student's concept will be different and unique.

✏ Pull up a weed and draw its roots, stem, and leaves. Imagine a root system of a large tree. It is at least as large as the tree. Draw your idea of a tree's roots. This is a drawing of trees clinging to rocks near the ocean. Notice how the wind has blown the branches.

5. Drawing Textures

✏ Look for interesting weeds. Milkweed pods are great examples, especially after they have dried and the pods have burst open. Try to draw the rough texture of the pods and the fine lines of the seeds. Think of different kinds of lines you can use to show rough texture, such as many tiny lines massed together or many dots. Try doing a rubbing on a rough surface. This is an ink drawing of a milkweed pod. Imagine where all the seeds will land as they blow away. Write about it.

✏ Look closely at dandelions—especially when they have exploded into balls of white seeds. Did you know that the word *dandelion* is from the French expression *dent de lion*, which means "lion's tooth"? How is a dandelion like a lion's tooth? Write about it.

✏ Feel the brittle texture of the layers that protect the seeds of a pine cone. Study the way its parts spread out and overlap. Draw a pine cone. Start at one end and just keep your eye on each part as you draw it. Draw slowly and thoughtfully. Write about how the seeds in the pine cones are spread around to start new trees.

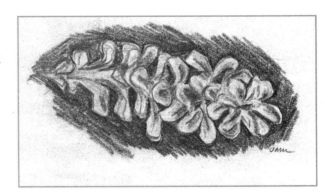

✏ Draw the back of another student's hair. Find every line—straight, curly, wavy, long, and short. Fill your paper with lines. Then write about what else your drawing could be.

✏ Draw a fuzzy toy. Decide what kind of lines you could use to show the fuzzy texture. *(Point out that texture in the drawing should cover the whole surface, not just the outline.)* Think of good adjectives to describe textures. List them. This is a student's drawing.

6. Drawing Food

Bring fresh vegetables and fruits to class. Bunches of carrots, endive or leaf lettuces, bunches of radishes or individual radishes with their leaves, pears, apples, bananas, and bunches of grapes have interesting shapes. Take time to talk about them and look carefully at shapes, colors, and textures.

- Carrots are a root vegetable. *(Display a carrot with its roots.)* Notice all the tiny roots growing from the carrot. How can you draw the fine lines of carrot leaves? Draw a bunch of carrots. Write about how you might prepare carrots for eating.

Connect the next exercise to a science lesson about nutrition. Ask students to select one thing for each category and draw it.

- Draw the parts of the food pyramid: dairy products, grains, fruit and vegetables, and protein—meat, fish, eggs. Choose your favorite thing in each section. Write about planning a balanced meal.

- Draw a broccoli cluster. How can you show the texture of the flower part of the broccoli? This student used a piece of sponge and ink. Do you like broccoli? It is very nutritious. Write about broccoli.

- Draw your lunch before you eat it. Then draw the remains at the end of lunch—banana peels, crumpled paper, and so on. Write about conserving food.

From works by Stacie Downs, Molly Headley, Sarah Engelbach, Sheila McCarroll

✏ Draw ears of corn. Draw one before you peel back the layers that protect it. Draw it again as you peel it. Write about your favorite corn dish. This drawing of ears of corn is by artist Joyce Kuhlmann Rebora. Notice all the lines she left in and drew over.

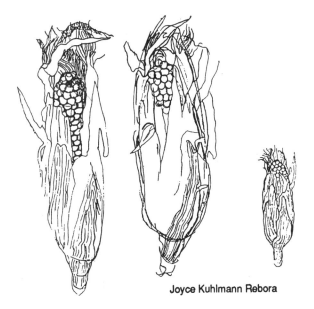

Joyce Kuhlmann Rebora

✏ Study the round shape of an orange. Look at the stem and the bottom. How can you show the rough texture of the orange peel? Draw a group of three oranges. Write about how you peel an orange.

✏ Draw a greatly enlarged strawberry. Think about its leafy stem and the tiny seeds all over its surface that resemble straws. What is your favorite way to eat strawberries? Write about it.

7. Cutting Letters and Inventing New Shapes

The cutting of shapes with scissors is a powerful learning device that develops eye-hand coordination. This skill provides many possibilities for learning in the classroom. For instance, cutting letters of the alphabet is a way to involve your students in every bulletin board in the room. Cut strips of 12" × 18" construction paper into 4" × 18" strips. Give each student a strip and a pair of scissors.

✏ Cut from your strip a piece the width of the letter you want to create. *M* and *W* and round letters such as *O, G, Q,* and *D* will need a wider strip than *A* or *E.* Look at the piece you have cut as a box that contains that letter. Cut away the outside, keeping a straight edge like the line of a *B* or a *K.* Then cut away to make a thin or a thick letter. Pierce the center of a closed shape with the point of the scissors and cut out the inside shape.

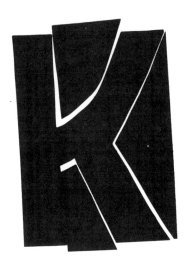

Start a bulletin-board word tile game with the cut letters. Put the letters in a box at the base of an empty board. Invite students to make words with the letters. If they need a letter, they can cut it. Pin or staple the words on the board and invite students to build on the words in a horizontal and vertical pattern.

Begin an adjective board. Once students can visualize letters and cut them out, ask them to design the letters so they look like the words they represent. Have each student cut out one adjective and attach it to a bulletin board. Leave the display on the board. Invite students to create more adjectives during free moments. Continue for a few weeks until the board is filled.

When the board is filled with adjectives, you can start a story on a long piece of mural paper that has been folded into a large accordion-fold book. Invite students who have finished their work to use adjectives from the board to write a story in large letters with black marker. Each time they use an adjective, have them remove it from the board and glue it into the story. Continue developing the story until all the adjectives are used.

✏ Create a verb board, a noun board, a participle board, and so on.

8. Cutting Names

The exercise that follows makes an excellent activity for the first day of school. Students learn how to cut letters, decorate the room, and feel ownership. You learn all their names!

✏ Cut the letters of your name so that they look like you—tall, thin, funny, graceful, and so on. Glue the letters on a 12" × 18" sheet of construction paper and draw some things you like around your name.

✏ Fold a piece of 9" × 12" construction paper lengthwise. In large letters, write your first name along the fold. Then cut out the outline of your name, keeping the fold intact. Glue the cut design on another sheet of paper and decorate it.

9. Cutting Math Shapes

Teach the concept of **positive/negative**. Distribute
3" squares of black construction paper. Ask
students to cut out shapes from the square so that
the square is still there. Have them start at one
side of the square and return to the same side.
When they have finished, mount all of the pieces
in a checkerboard positive/negative pattern on a
bulletin board.

✏ *(Prepare and distribute 3" wide strips of
constructia paper in a variety of colors.)*
Cut many geometric shapes from 1" to
3"—triangles, squares, long thin
rectangles, circles, and so on. Combine
the shapes into a collage of people dancing. Take time to try different
arrangements. When you are satisfied with the arrangement, glue the
shapes carefully in place.

✏ *(Distribute sheets of 9" x 12" construction paper.)* Measure and cut out a 9"
square. Mark the midpoint of each side of the square and draw a
straight line from one mark to another to make another square. Then
mark the midpoint of each side of this square and draw another square.
Use crayons to draw repeated patterns in the triangles that you formed.

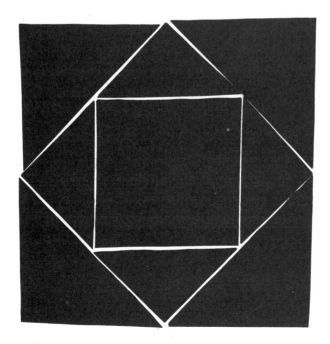

✏ Fold a 9" × 12" sheet of construction paper in half. On the fold, cut the shape of a bilaterally symmetrical mask. Cut geometric shapes into the mask to make the nose, eyes, and mouth. Give your mask a name and a purpose. Write about it.

*Explain that **tessellations** are shapes that have no space between them when repeated. Square tiles can form tessellations. This exercise starts with a square and, by shifting parts, creates a repeated pattern design. It is important to stress accuracy in tracing.*

✏ Cut a tessellation shape and repeat it into a full-page design. Start with a 2" square. *(Display the diagram below and demonstrate each step.)* (1) Cut a shape from one side. (2) Slide this shape to the opposite side of the square and tape the uncut edges together. (3) Cut a shape from another side. (4) Slide this shape to the opposite side and tape the uncut edges together. Then trace the shape carefully in the upper left corner of your sketchbook page. Move the pattern to the right. The tessellated shape will fit exactly into your first tracing. Fill the page with the shape, using the traced edge each time to start a new shape. When you have filled the page, look at your shape and find an image in it. Add details to make it into a figure, a bird, or whatever you would like it to be.

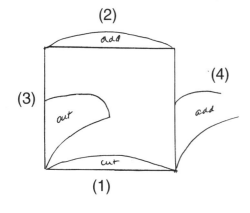

10. Learning Composition

Composition *means the arrangement of forms. A good composition should include the following principles of art.*

Balance. *Balance can be symmetrical or asymmetrical. Bilaterally symmetrical means the composition has equally sized shapes on each side of its center.*

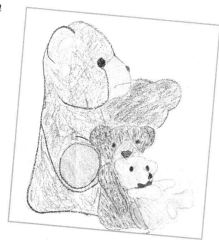

Proportion and Variety. *The relation of shapes and colors to each other in a composition can be realistically proportional or exaggerated. A variety of lines, shapes, and colors adds interest to a composition.*

Rhythm. *In art, rhythm is an ordered movement created by the repetition of color, shape, line, and other elements of art.*

Foreground and Background. *Foreground is the space in the front of an artwork. Background is the space behind the foreground. In a landscape, background is marked by a* **horizon line**. *In a room, it may be the floor line at the wall. In a still-life drawing, the background is the space behind the objects.*

Overlapping. *Objects in a composition can be drawn overlapping, with one behind another.*

Set up a still life arrangement. This means a group of objects placed together. Set it in the center of the room so that everyone can see it from a different angle. These drawings of an arrangement of teddy bears were done from different angles.

Asymmetry means balance that is not evenly placed. A large object might be balanced by a few small ones. Lines moving across the drawing help to create a balance too.

- Draw a vase of flowers on one side of your paper. Then fill in the background with lines, shapes, and patterns to complete your composition with asymmetrical balance. Describe how and why your drawing is balanced and pleasing.

- Draw a bilaterally symmetrical composition. Draw a tree in the center of your paper. Then draw smaller trees on each side of it. Fill your drawing with bushes and trees, always adding the same size and shape to each side. Describe how you would plan a park and plant trees in it.

- Notice how the diagonal shape in this student's still life drawing leads your eye to the right. Plan an arrangement of shoes, gloves, a school bag, a hat, a scarf, or other objects. Place the objects in an arrangement you like and draw what you see. Make up a story about the arrangement.

11. Composing with Imaginary Lines

✏ Think about a tornado's spiral form. It is large at the top but narrows as it nears the ground. Use crayon colors that look like a tornado and draw many lines that show wind and rain. Fill your paper to make a pleasing composition. Write a poem about a tornado.

✏ Start at any point on the edge of your paper. Draw a crayon line that wanders wherever you want it to go but ends up at another edge. Draw five or six more lines using different colors and thicknesses. As you draw your lines, try to create good balance and rhythm on your paper. Write about taking a walk.

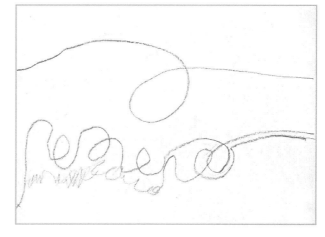

✏ Imagine the wind as a face blowing. Make your own idea of wind blowing. Fill your paper with an interesting composition. Write what the wind might be saying.

12. Composing with the Tools of Math

The ruler, compass, and protractor are good tools for drawing. Students can develop their skills in measuring and manipulating the tools when using them to draw.

Set up two mirrors, each at a 60-degree angle. Use duct tape to attach them and a protractor to measure. Ask students to cut shapes from construction paper and experiment with designs. Each design will reflect into a hexagonal pattern in the mirrors.

- Make a mirror kaleidoscope. When you are satisfied with your design, cut six of each shape, arrange the pieces in a hexagonal pattern, and glue in place. Write about places you might find hexagons *(hornets' nests, honey combs, floor tiles, geodesic domes).*

Do directed drawings with pencils and rulers. The exercise that follows is one example. Continue with other directed lines. If students have compasses, you might include circles. Ask students to decide what they have drawn and have them write about it.

- Draw a 6" vertical line on your paper. Exactly 3" below the vertical line, draw a 4" diagonal line. On another sheet of paper, draw a 2" square. Below it draw three 3" lines.

- Draw a large circle. Draw smaller concentric circles from the same center point. Draw repeated pattern designs in each section. Use markers to give your design strength. Write about three circular objects that you use at school or at home. *(This is a student's example.)*

✏ Use a ruler and a compass to draw lines that divide the space on the sketchbook page. Fill in the sections with more straight lines or patterns in many colors of marker. Write your own version of the directions for this exercise.

✏ Use a compass to draw a circle with a radius of two inches. Place your compass point on the perimeter of the circle and draw another circle. Draw six circles around the center circle. Then complete your design with more small circles. This is a fourth grader's example.

✏ Use a concentric pattern of fourths in a design.

These are two students' examples.

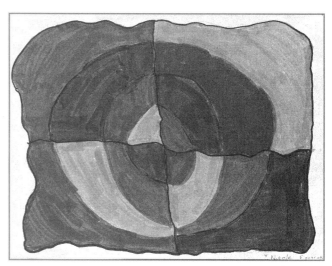

13. Composing on a Computer

Computer drawing programs are very useful for developing awareness of line quality, direction, and tone. Using different software options, students can experiment with thick and thin lines, varied directions, repetition of lines and shapes, composition, and tonality. Here are two beginning exercises.

✏ Use many different kinds of lines to make a pleasing composition in a computer drawing program. Repeat lines and shapes to create rhythm. Try to achieve balance—either symmetrical or asymmetrical—in your composition. Look at the proportions of large and small forms. *(This is a student's example.)*

✏ Experiment with wash tones using a computer drawing program to learn about shadow effects. Combine lines and washes in a composition.

14. Drawing the Human Figure

This skill is essential. Do not accept stick figures. Once your students feel confident posing for each other and drawing gestures, you can apply this skill to the expression of any and all of their studies. Here are some things to look for when you critique students' figure drawings.

Proportion/Size and Relation of Parts.
Is the head too large for the body? Are the arms long enough? Do the elbows come to the waist? How far down do the hands reach? The better students understand the way their bodies work, the better they will be able to draw them.

Take Some Measurements.
Most adult bodies are about seven heads high. Children's bodies are much less than that. Measure your model's head and then see how many heads tall he or she is.

Details.
Did students draw hands and feet? In a full contour drawing, did they draw features in the face and details of clothing?

Movement.
Do students' figures look as if they could move an arm or a leg? Are they too stiff?

Line.
Did students hatch their lines instead of letting them flow? Remind them to let their lines follow the path of their eyes.

Use a cardboard Halloween skeleton or a small plastic model to study the structure of the human body. Show students the skeleton's head and how the neck continues into the backbone as well as the shoulder bones. Show the two straight arm bones with ball joints at the shoulders. You might compare the way this joint moves to the way a joystick moves. Have students demonstrate that their elbows come to their waists and their hands to their mid-thighs. Point out the skeleton's hipbones and the two straight leg bones connected to the hip with ball joints. Have students feel these bones in their own bodies.

✏ Do a gesture drawing from a posed model and fill in the bones. Think about the skull, backbone, ribs, shoulder bones, hipbones, joints, hands, and feet. Describe how the body moves, the marvelous way our bones and muscles allow us to do so many things. This student's example was done on black paper with cotton swabs.

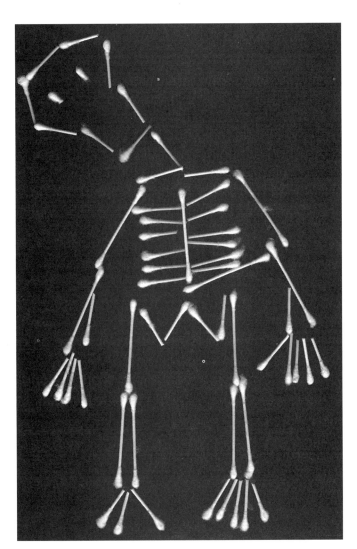

Gesture Drawing

*To do **gesture drawings**, tell students to look only at the outline of the body, not the details. Start with a student model in front of the room taking a simple pose with arms akimbo (hands on hips and elbows bent outward) or one akimbo and one upraised. Direct students to start with the oval of the head. Use practice paper for students' first gesture drawings.*

✐ Keeping your eyes on the model, follow the line from the head to one side of the neck, to the shoulder, to the arm—both straight sections— around the hand, up the inside of the arm to the body, down to the waist, to the hip, to the knee, to the foot, and up the inside of the leg. Continue around the body until your line reaches the other side of the neck.

  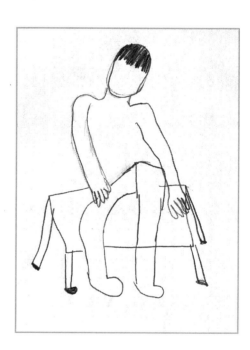

Do many gesture sketches, taking time to look at the results for proportions and body parts. Keep to frontal poses until students are comfortable with the figure. Point out that students on opposite sides of the room will see the model differently. Change models for each pose.

✏ *(Have your model play "Statue Maker" and freeze in a good action pose.)* Draw the pose and then describe what your model might be doing.

Have your models pose in good and bad postures. Have students look at the position of the backbone. Is it straight or slouched? Connect this to health and physical education lessons. Have students write about posture.

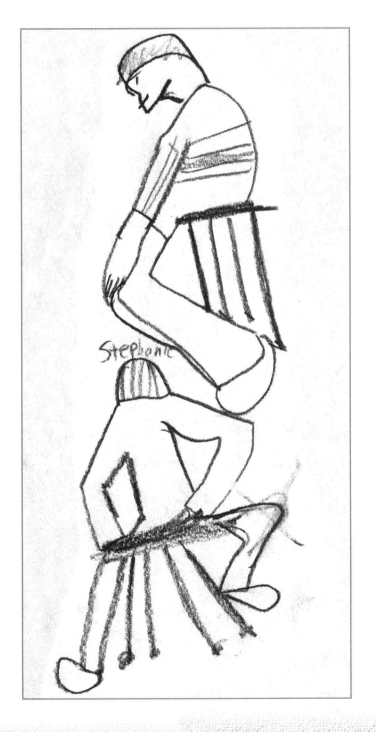

Stephanie

15. It Looks Different from Every Angle

✐ *(Position your model in the center of the room so students can see the pose from all different angles.)* Draw the model. Compare views when you have finished. Write about how you saw the model. These students' drawings show three views of the same model.

16. Drawing Parts You Can't See

Have models sit on a chair, stand at a chair with one foot on the seat, or sit on the floor. Ask students to think of a pose that hides some parts of the model from view.

✏ How do you draw a head or a body that is bent or turned around? Or an arm that is behind the body or bent away from you? Trust your eyes. Draw only what you see. Do many poses like this. Write about what you learn.

✏ Try drawing a back view. *(Pose your model sitting or standing on a chair with his or her back to the class.)* Draw as much of the model's legs, arms, and face as you see from your view.

17. Capturing Action

✏ Your models won't always be sitting or standing still for you. Let's look at models that are moving. How can your lines capture that movement? Draw your models in action, like dancing. Try to show the movement with your lines and shapes.

✏ Have a model pose in four stages of a movement. Draw all four poses in sequence to show the action. Write about what you learned from doing this.

✏ Have your models pose in gestures suggesting emotions— excitement, fear, or anger. Think of other emotions. Write about what the person in your drawing is thinking.

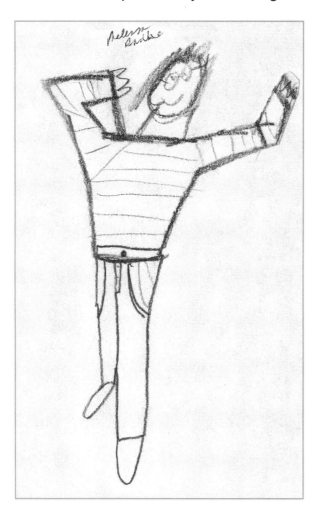

18. Drawing Faces

Teach the proportions of the face. Begin by drawing an oval on the board. Then measure the oval from top to bottom and draw a line across the midpoint. Help students discover that the eyes are in the middle of the skull and that the ears are level with the eyes. Have students come up and draw eyes, eyebrows, ears, a nose, a mouth, and the hairline. Then measure a young child's face and point out that the proportions are different—the eyes are much lower and the forehead is larger.

✏ Face a partner and draw a front view of his or her face.

1. Start with the oval of the head. Look at the chin line. Is it pointed, round, or square?

2. Measure from the top of the head to the chin and lightly mark the halfway point. Draw the eyes here. Look at the eyelids and eyelashes. Look closely at the iris of each eye. The eyelid will cover about a third of the eye unless the person is staring wide-eyed. Draw the pupils of the eyes.

3. Draw the eyebrows. Feel on your own face how your eyebrows lead to the nose. The nose will come about halfway down the lower half of the face. Draw the nostrils and the end of the nose.

4. Draw the mouth.

5. Draw the ears. They are even or level with the eyes.

6. Draw the hairline and the shape of the hair.

7. Finally, draw the neck and shoulders.

faces, looking each time at details and proportions.
ır model's features.

✏ Ask students to pose with facial expressions of fear, excitement, anger, joy, and so on. Point out how the features change. Draw and write about the expressions. Here is a student's example.

✏ Draw your self-portrait. Look in a mirror and find the shape of your face, the lines of your eyebrows, your hairline, the style of your hair, and so on. Create a verbal self-portrait by describing yourself in words.

19. Drawing Body Details

✏️ Draw your hand from two views. Put your thumb and index finger together for one view. Write about all the things that pressing these two fingers together allows you to do.

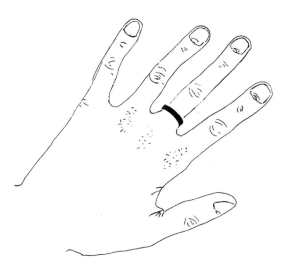

✏️ Look down at your leg and foot. Draw your leg and foot with your shoe and sock on. Write about how your shoe feels to the touch.

✏️ Look carefully at the ear of the student next to you. Draw the ear with every detail. Let your eye follow each line and curve. Write about your favorite sounds.

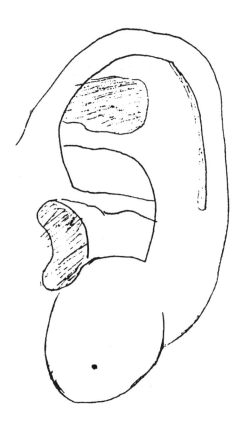

20. Contour Drawing

Discuss with students the importance of trusting their own vision and not trying to draw like someone else. Remind them to just keep trying to see better and to draw what they see. You might have students write this in their journals. Then, discuss the confidence that each student should have in his or her own work.

✏ Now that you have drawn the gestures of the body and the way its parts move together, you are ready to see the figure as artists see it—finding all the edges as they move across the body, with some edges disappearing and others crossing over them. You are now ready to do contour drawing of figures. *(You might ask students to write the following in their journals for reference.)*

Contour drawing is a very sensitive search for all the lines you can see. Let your eye follow the line of the collar, the folds and creases of the clothing, the lines of the face and hair. Do contour drawing more slowly than gesture drawing. Enjoy all the lines and the way they disappear as another fold overlaps them. Think of contour drawing as if you are walking across a landscape with hills and valleys. Your eyes find "paths," and your pencil records them.

✏ Take some time to "draw with your finger." Look at the model and, with one eye closed, trace the edges you see with your finger. Follow the line of a collar around the neck and to the front. Find the lines of folds, pleats, and decorations on the model's clothes. Then draw as your eyes "feel" each line. Write about the path your eye took. This is a student's example of contour drawing.

✏ This contour line drawing is by German artist Lovis Corinth. Study all
the lines that show both form and shadow.

21. Drawing Groups

This is another important concept. Gather photographs or magazine pictures and spend time looking at the way figures overlap. Note that the figures in the background appear smaller as they go back in the picture. The goals of these exercises are figure drawing, perspective through overlapping of forms, reduced size of objects in the distance, and composition.

✏ Ask three students to pose in a group. All the students can stand, or one can sit with the other students standing behind him or her. Draw them as a group, drawing only what you see of the person or persons in the back. Write a news story about an important meeting.

*Teach **horizon line**—the line that separates the floor or ground from the background. When drawing people in a room, their feet should be below the floor line. This very quick sketch was done as students stood around a table planning a project.*

✏ Draw people working together—men repairing a road, carpenters, or firefighters. Think of several more. Pose, draw, and write about the job being done.

✏ *(Suggest that your models take action poses of what might happen at a baseball game.)* Draw the details as well as the action—the uniforms, the bat, and so on. Pretend you are a reporter at the game. Write about the action you see.

✏ *(Collect photographs of basketball games and have students study the way players overlap and the way they vary in size as they are nearer to the camera.)* Using a large sheet of paper (18" × 24"), compose a basketball game. Pretend you are a sports writer at a basketball game. Draw the basket wherever you wish—to the left or right side or in the center. Ask models to pose in positions that represent movements in a basketball game. As each model takes a pose, draw the pose wherever it fits in your composition. If one is behind another, draw only the part you see. You might also draw uniforms on the players. Place a floor line horizontally just above the highest placed figure. Add a background to your drawing. Now, write about the game.

✏ Draw your family as a group. Write about each person in the group.

✏ Draw a Thanksgiving Day celebration. You might draw the first Thanksgiving or your own family dinner. Write about the menu for the dinner.

22. Cutting Figures

Cutting is an excellent eye-hand coordination experience. Give students a 12" × 18" sheet of construction paper and scissors. Have a model face the class. Ask students to move so they will have a frontal view of the pose. Side views are difficult to cut. Show students how to start from the foot and cut up while holding the paper up in view of the model. Ask them to try to contain the entire figure in the 18" height. Encourage students to add details of feet and hands—no gingerbread cookies! Ask students to look at their completed figures to see if they have cut the neck and shoulders, two parts of each arm, hands, and feet. Try to do this several times until all students seem to be catching on. Remind them of the importance of trying and learning from their mistakes. Consider making a bulletin board mural by arranging all of the figures together.

Cut figures from poses related to an event in history. Use 6" × 9" construction paper so figures will be small enough to place on an overhead projector. Use the overhead projector to enlarge the figures onto mural paper and plan a history mural. This kind of a class project can be started in a drawing/writing period and students can work on it over a period of time. Keep the overhead projector on hand so figures can be enlarged and traced. Details and background can be added with chalk, crayons, or tempera paint.

23. Animating Cut Figures

Pose a model in an action stance so that all students have a frontal view of the model. Distribute sheets of 6" x 9" paper. Have students look at the model. Tell them to hold up their papers and begin cutting out the model's pose starting at the model's foot, cutting up to the head and then around the other side. Next, distribute sheets of 12" x 18" construction paper. Tell students to move the cut figure around on the construction paper until they decide on an action to show. Demonstrate how to trace the figure many times to create a strobe-like action. You can draw the tracings in **transparency,** *which means that the entire figure is drawn each time, allowing it to show through the figure in front of it; you can trace the figures so that they overlap and seem to be behind one another, as is shown in the drawing below; or you can invent your own way of doing it. When students have finished tracing, have them glue their cut figures onto their drawings.*

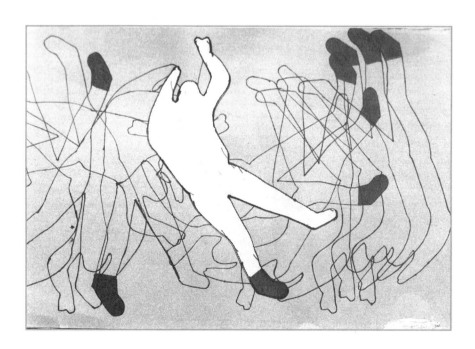

✏ Cut figures in dancing poses. Arrange them into a bulletin board mural. Write about the music that you think the figures hear. Is it fast or slow?

24. Finding Subjects in Your Studies

Bring in clothing that could be used as costumes for persons you are studying in social studies. Have a student pose in a gesture that expresses that person. Ask students to do contour drawings of the model and to write about this person's actions. This drawing was done from a male model who posed for the class in a Civil War uniform.

✏ Draw a book report instead of writing it. Have a friend pose for you in actions that depict the characters in the book. Add the background and other details.

Bring in costumes of your ethnic traditions and pose for the class. Tell stories about the costume and your family's traditions. Have students write about the traditions.

Illustrate a story or legend from the ethnic or cultural tradition of some of your students. Have students write about it.

Study Egyptian tomb paintings and relief sculpture. Relief means that the figures are carved only about an inch deep into the wall. Relief sculpture is the opposite of sculpture in the round or the carving of a full figure that you can see from all sides. Egyptian artists drew figures with the broadest view of each part facing front so the head is in profile (side view), the shoulders and body are front facing, and the legs are drawn from the side. This is a section of a wall relief carving from the Egyptian temple in Dendera. Have students draw figures in the Egyptian style as other students pose in these positions.

✏ What would you like to be when you grow up? Draw a future self-portrait in the setting of your occupation. Write about your ambition.

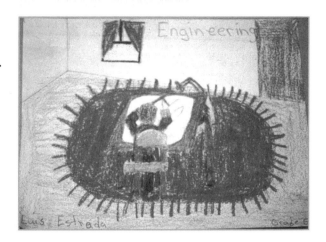

✏ How do people who live in different climates within the United States dress? *(Pose a model who is dressed for a special climate or time of year.)* Draw the model in his or her clothing. Here is a student's drawing of two climate zones.

At the end of the school year, assign each chapter of your history or social studies textbook to a different pair of students. Ask them to reread the chapter, find people and events that are important, and take turns posing while one draws the other.

✏ Write a brief summary of the event or person you drew. Make a booklet about the chapter. Here is an example—a group of students posed for each other and drew this scene showing the traditional way of life of some Native Americans.

25. Drawing Animals

Drawing animals, birds, fish, and insects helps students understand their structure and body parts. It also connects directly to your science curriculum. Build up a collection of photographs and make them available to your students to study carefully. Use encyclopedias, the Internet, National Geographic *films, and so on to observe both the structure and movement of animals.*

Encourage your students to draw animals in the same way they draw objects and figures— letting their eyes direct their hands. Have them use simple flowing lines that express shape and movement.

✏ Prehistoric artists drew the animals they hunted on the walls of caves. Look at photos of animals and draw only the big movements you see. Write about how cave people hunted animals.

✏ *(Distribute brown kraft paper cut into 12" × 18" pieces.)* Crumple your paper and then smooth it out. It will look rough like the surface of a cave wall. Use a brush and black ink to draw an animal as the cave artists did. These are students' examples of an elephant and a deer.

✏ Many animals in the jungle have protective coloration, or **camoflauge,** that helps to hide them from predators or to stalk their prey. Draw an animal, such as a tiger, and draw lines of tall grass that blend in with its stripes to hide it. Use the word *camouflage* in sentences about animals.

✏ Fold a piece of 6" × 9" paper in half. On the inside fold, draw a picture of an animal. On the front fold, write three sentences describing your animal. Exchange folded papers with a partner and see if you can guess what the animal is before looking at the drawing.

✏ Draw animals you see in the zoo. List all the physical characteristics you can think of for the animal. This is a student's drawing of a gorilla.

✏ Use a black marker to draw a design based on the stripes of a zebra or the spots of a leopard. Fill your paper as if you were doing a close-up of a zebra or a leopard.

✏ Tear construction paper into the shape of a zoo animal. Glue the torn piece onto your sketchbook page. Add lines to finish the animal.

✏ This drawing of a horse is by German artist Lovis Corinth. Notice how the lines "search" for the shape of the horse. He often drew three or four lines. Look at the background. The lines for the fence and the background seem to be a "search." Draw a picture like this one.

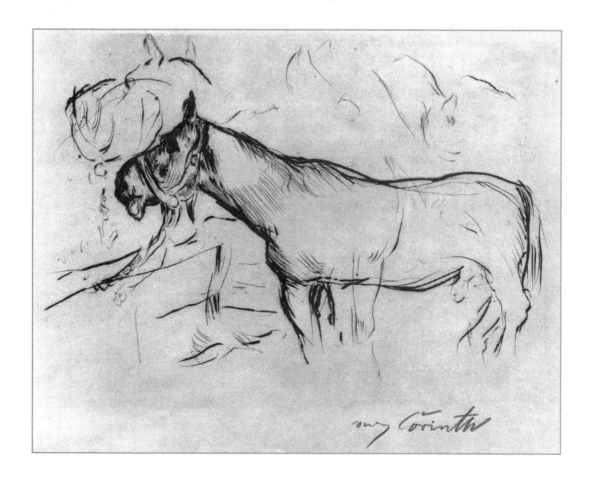

26. Drawing Birds

✏ Use films or videos to study the shape and movement of birds. This line drawing of a white egret was done in a bird sanctuary in Florida. Use a fine-line marker and follow the graceful lines of the neck and the delicate tail feathers of birds. Write about where your bird lives.

✏ Draw a tree filled with birds. Use crayons and many colors to draw many kinds of birds. Write a poem about your tree.

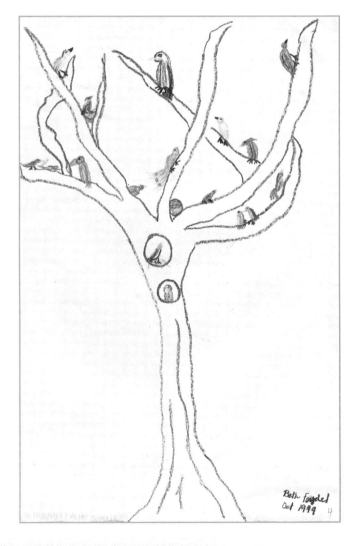

✏ Draw your pet bird or animal. If you do not have a pet, draw one you would like to have. Write about it. These are side and back views of a student's pet bird.

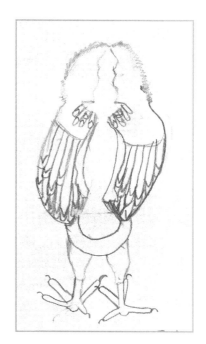

✏ This design of birds and a wonderful tree was done in a scratchboard technique. The paper was first heavily colored with brightly colored crayons. Then black ink was painted over it. The drawing was made by scratching away the ink and showing the color under it. Use a scratchboard technique to draw a design of birds.

27. Drawing Fish and Other Sea Creatures

You might correlate these drawing exercises with science lessons that discuss the structure and characteristics of fish and sea creatures. Look for the common body parts they share and the limitless variety in different kinds of sea creatures. Look for pattern and color on the bodies of fish.

✏ Draw a sea full of fish. Draw seaweed and other sea plants. Write a poem about your sea. This is a fourth grader's drawing.

✏ Draw sharks, whales, or other large sea creatures swimming in the ocean. This is a student's drawing. Write about one of the creatures in your drawing and what it eats.

With a fine-line marker, draw five fish shapes on your paper. Then start at the left edge and draw lines across your paper to represent water. Let the lines curve around the fish. Fill your paper with these lines. How would you like to live in water? Tell about it.

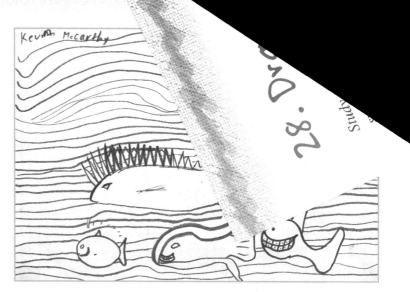

Find some leaves that look like the shape of fish and glue them to a background. Use crayons to add color and draw seaweed to make an underwater scene. Write a haiku about your scene. A haiku is a Japanese poem with three lines: the first line has five syllables, the second line has seven syllables, and the third line has five syllables. *(Read the following poem aloud.)*

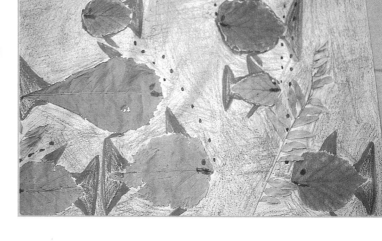

Leaves fall from the sky

Float into my waterland

Becoming fine fish

Learn about a particular species of fish from an encyclopedia, a library reference book, or the Internet. Draw a picture of the fish, and be sure to add all its special characteristics. Write about what you learned.

Drawing Insects

the structure of an insect's body—the symmetry, the number of legs, and the parts of the body—head, antennae, thorax, abdomen, wings, and legs. Find photographs of many species or obtain a display from a local natural history museum.

3| Katrina 103|
dragon Flys in the air are eme were. Here and there are dragon flys every were, dragon fly dragon Fly

- Draw a dragonfly with its long body, two pairs of wings, antennae, and legs. Write a poem about how it flies. This is a student's drawing.

- Draw a caterpillar. Draw many segments of its body with a pair of legs for each segment. Is your caterpillar fuzzy? Is it brightly colored? Is it striped or spotted? Draw it a second time in its cocoon, waiting to emerge as a butterfly. Write about metamorphosis.

- Look at photographs of butterflies and notice that the wing patterns are bilaterally symmetrical, or mirror reflections of each other. Use crayons to make a beautifully colored butterfly. Fill your page with a large drawing. Using colorful adjectives, write a description of your butterfly.

- Look for insects on the Internet or in encyclopedias. Draw all of the parts of an insect. Write about how many insects you can recognize.

- Draw five small insects on your sketchbook page. Now draw tall grass, leaves, and flowers so that the insects can hide as they do in a garden. This is called camouflage. Find out about insects that look like leaves or twigs.

How many legs does a spider have? Learn about the spider's body parts. Draw a spider and its web. Note the radial symmetry of the web. Write a conversation between a spider and a fly with the spider inviting the fly into its web.

29. Drawing Architecture

Buildings are so large that it seems daunting to try to draw them. For classroom reference, bring several books on architecture from the library. Take your students outside with sketchbooks and pencils. Spend time looking at the school building or a house in the neighborhood. Ask students to note details—door, door frame, windows, roof lines, and so on. When students draw buildings, have them start with the door and work out from it, one detail at a time.

✏️ Draw the front of your home or apartment building from memory. Think about the doorway, stairs, windows, and roof lines. When you get home, do another drawing while you are looking at your home. Compare the drawings. Write a description of your home. These are students' drawings of a house and an apartment building.

Make a vocabulary list of structural forms— **arch, lintel, column, capital, eaves, dormer window, pediment, tower, cupola, spire, buttress,** *and so on. Define the vocabulary words for students.*

✏️ Draw pictures of each vocabulary word. This is a student's drawing of a tower.

✏ Draw a row of skyscrapers. Add rows of windows on each. This student drew the rooftops as if she were flying above the buildings. Plan your own way of showing a big city's skyline.

✏ This is a photograph of George Washington's home in Mt. Vernon. Study the symmetry of its design. Find the dormer windows, pediments, shutters, and the cupola. Draw your version of Mt. Vernon.

Showing Space in Drawings

✏ Draw your classroom windows and what you see from them. Note the size of houses and trees. Describe your view. These are students' drawings.

✏ Reducing the size of forms in the distance is a way to show space in the foreground of your drawing. Notice the small size of the building and the archway in the foreground of this drawing. Draw a building in the foreground of your picture. Then draw a road leading back and draw a house along the road. Make it smaller. This student drawing shows lots of houses getting smaller and smaller in the background.

✏ Another way to show space in a drawing is to overlap shapes in the background of the picture. Draw a city on a hill. Show the bottom row of houses and then the walls, windows, rooftops, chimneys, and trees as the town goes up the hill. Add spires, domes, and so on. Do you live on a hill? Write about what it is like (or what it would be like) to climb up and down the hill. This drawing was done in the Italian town of Tellaro.

30. Drawing Your Travels— Real or Wished For

✏ Study the architecture and natural forms of places you have learned about in geography. Research a place to which you would like to travel. Request travel brochures from travel agencies or tourist offices of foreign countries. Perhaps you can use the Internet to find out more about these places. This quick sketch is an example of how you can record your travels. It was done in the French town of St. Cirq Lapopie, in the Dordogne region of southwest France.

✏ Look at a photograph of a place you would like to visit. Find some part of it that you would like to draw. Look for the lines that make the shape of what you want to draw. Then add details as you see them. Read about the place and write a description of it.

✏ Find out about the shapes of homes in different parts of the world. Draw a picture of a home from an African village. Most of these homes are circular and have conical roofs. Write about the building materials that are used in this type of home.

✏ Research a place where you would like to travel. Design a poster advertising it. Write about its special features.

✏ Imagine traveling in a hot air balloon. Who will be with you? How does the balloon rise? Find out about it. Draw it. Design your balloon with wonderful colors and shapes. Write about where you are going and how it looks from above.

✏ Would you like to go skiing? Draw a scene of snow-covered hills and skiers. Start at the bottom of your paper and build up overlapping hills. Write a poem about skiing.

✏ How else can you travel? Draw a huge airplane flying over a city or an ocean. What is it like to fly in a plane? Write about it. This is a student's drawing of an airplane ride.

✏ This is a drawing of the Badlands of South Dakota. The terrain is stark, with no trees, just rock mesas and **buttes**. Locate the Badlands on a map of the United States. Use the side of a pencil to draw the shapes of rock formations like these. Write about being lost in the Badlands.

31. Drawing Maps

✏ City maps are designs for living. This is a section of a map of Cologne, Germany. *(Locate Cologne on a map of Germany.)* See how the streets curve into the path of the river. Obtain a map of a city you would like to visit. Study its street patterns— note whether the streets follow a grid pattern, curve around a river, follow a radial pattern, or something else. Select a section of the city and draw the pattern of the streets. Write what you learned about your city.

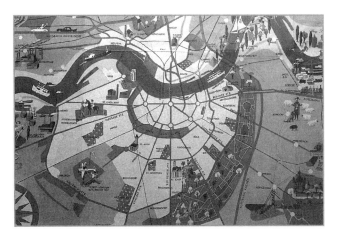

✏ Design your own city map. Will your streets follow a grid pattern or a circular pattern? Some cities are designed with streets radiating out from a center point. In Washington, D.C., for example, the main streets radiate from the Capitol building. If a river runs through your city, the streets might follow its curve. Write about your city after you have finished designing it. This is a student's map.

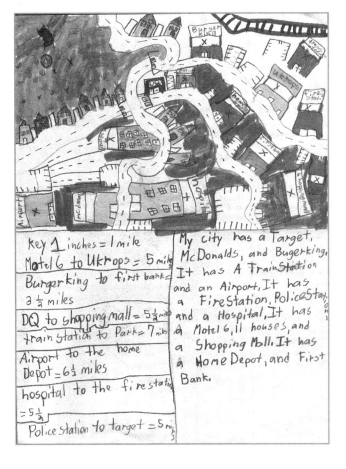

There are many different kinds of maps. If you were a farmer, you would map out your farmland and plan where to plant each crop. Farmers are like designers when they plow their land. Divide your page into farm plots. "Plow" each section with repeated lines to use up all of your land. Write about your crops. This is one student's design.

Astronomers map the stars and planets. They have named many constellations, or groups of stars, such as the Big Dipper, the Little Dipper, Ursa the Bear, and Orion the Hunter. Glue five or six stars on your sketchbook page. Then draw lines to connect them and see what you can make. These students found "A Howling Wolf" and "Big Rocket in the Sky." Write a description of your constellation.

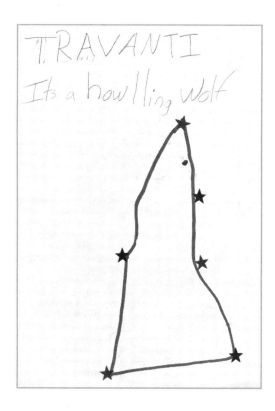

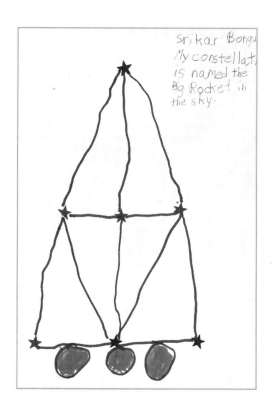

✏️ Exploding stars are called *novas*. This student drew five dots on paper and then made them "explode." Try it yourself. Use several crayon colors and draw lines around the dots in concentric circles to look like explosions. Find out about novas and write about them.

32. Drawing from Imagination

Imaginative thinking and expressing is essential to learning. It frees students to make new connections, see relationships, and invent new ideas. The following exercises are designed to stimulate this kind of thinking. Be open to your students' ideas. Encourage fantasizing, exaggerating, and combining forms. If your students have ideas for drawing and writing exercises, listen to them and use them.

✏ Transform something in your classroom into a bird. Write about it. Here is a student's idea of a scissors bird.

✏ Suppose one day you wake up to find everything the wrong size. Draw what you see and write about it.

✏ Transform a piece of fruit or a vegetable into a vehicle. Describe how it would run and where it would go.

✏ Draw a figure from a posed model and exaggerate a movement by enlarging or extending a body part. Can you draw a figure that looks nervous?

✏ Design the letters of your name into funny creatures. Here is a student's example.

✏ Draw your shoe and transform it into a person or an animal. Describe its actions. This student's shoe became a stingray.

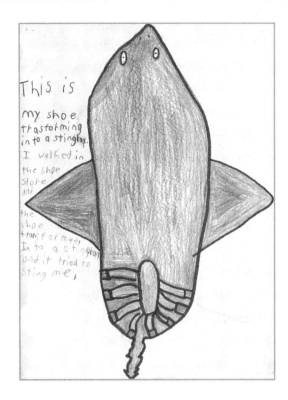

✏ *(Distribute sheets of paper.)* Start a drawing of a fantastic machine. After one minute, pass the paper to the next student. Ask that student to continue the drawing. Do this for seven or eight minutes, passing the drawing on to another student each minute. Then return the drawing to the student who started it. Now look at what your drawing has become. Decide what kind of a machine it is and write about it.

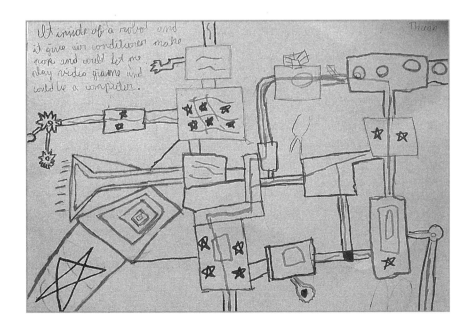

✏ Draw your self-portrait as your favorite food. Explain why it is your favorite. This student made her face into rice, her nose into a slice of tomato, and her eyes into potatoes.

✏ Invent a fantastic huge bird. Draw it. This one was done in scratchboard technique. The paper was covered with bright crayon. Black ink was painted over the crayon and a sharp tool was used to scratch the drawing. Notice the castle in the background.

✏ Draw a group of clowns. Give them funny faces, clothes, names, and personalities.

33. Encouraging Drawing at Home

The following pages offer many ideas for self-directed drawing at home. Allow students to take their sketchbooks home, or suggest that they keep another sketchbook at home.

Encouraging students to draw at home has many advantages, starting with the possibility of weaning them away from television and computer games. Students who develop a habit of drawing will not only enjoy it, they will build confidence that will last a lifetime. Give students credit for drawings done at home. Take time to look at them and, once in a while, display some "home" themes such as My Family, Kitchen Shapes, Pets, and so on.

You may want to duplicate pages 90 through 92 and send them home with your students. Encourage your students to add to the list ideas they have for drawings.

Drawing at Home

- Keep a special home sketchbook and find things in your home, in your neighborhood, and in your travels to fill your book. Take it with you on a family outing. Look for interesting things to draw.

- Draw some kitchen gadgets—can openers, scissors, peelers, ladles, spatulas, whisks, and so on.

- Pile up some pots and pans and draw the pile.

- Draw pieces of fruit and vegetables. Draw a banana. Then peel it halfway and draw it again. After you eat it, draw the peel.

- Draw a chair from the front, side, and top view, and at floor level.

- On a large cardboard box, plan a neighborhood. Draw buildings, trees, and stores on all sides.

- Draw your family members while they are working or while they are relaxing and watching TV. (You can get lots of drawing done during commercials!)

- Draw pictures of your family members doing what they do to help around the house, such as cooking, cleaning, and taking out the garbage.

- Draw your closet. Follow the lines of each thing hanging in it, the rows of pants, and so on.

- Draw a pair of your boots or shoes.

- Draw the view from a window in your house.

- Draw flowers in your garden or potted plants in your home.

✐ Draw your bicycle. On a sunny day, stand it in the sun. Place a large sheet of paper on the ground in the shadow of your bicycle and trace the shadow. Work quickly—if you work too slowly, the shadow will change!

✐ Draw your pets. Do many views of the pet—lying down, moving, eating, and so on. This is a student's drawing of what her future dog might be like.

✐ Draw your room. Look for all the details.

✐ Draw the trees that are in your neighborhood.

✐ Lie on your stomach in the grass. Look closely at the blades of grass and the dandelions or other plants growing there. Do a drawing of every blade of grass you see. If you do one blade at a time, it is not hard to do the whole thing.

✐ How do you dress when you are in a gym, at the beach, at a costume carnival, or at school? Draw yourself in any environment you choose. Have a friend pose for you in the action you want. Complete the figure by adding the kind of clothes that you need in such an environment. Complete the background.

✐ Draw flakes of cereal, like these, on a newspaper sheet. Look for every curve and bump.

✐ Use the financial or classified pages of a newspaper for a drawing. Draw some flowers using a black marker.

✐ Stand in front of a bright light to make a shadow on the opposite wall. Experiment with the lamp. The closer to the lamp you stand, the larger your shadow will be. The closer you come to the wall, the smaller your shadow will be. What will happen if the lamp is on the floor? How will your shadow look if you bend to the floor?

91

- Draw your favorite game or sports equipment.

- Keep a "visual log." Every day, notice something about one place in your home. Write about it. After a week, draw that place. You will see it much better.

- Invite a friend over and pose for each other as characters from your favorite book. Find articles of clothing that could make costumes for the characters.

- Draw your family's car.

- Design the car of your dreams.

- Draw yourself in a Halloween costume.

- Draw a portrait of yourself in a huge hat. Fill the hat with fruit, flowers, or kitchen utensils.

- Sit on the floor near your kitchen table and draw what it looks like from there. Trust your eyes. See which way each line seems to go.

- Invent your own picture alphabet. Choose an image for each letter. First make a chart. Then write a story with your alphabet.

Glossary

arch - a curved half-round or half-oval shape, usually seen in architecture as a doorway or window frame and constructed of wedge-shaped masonry or solid wood pieces that exert pressure against a central keystone to hold them in place. (see *keystone*)

balance - a state of stability or equilibrium. In art, visual balance can be symmetrical or asymmetrical. It is achieved with color, shape, line, proportion, and so on.

bilateral symmetry - mirror or similar images on both sides of a central axis

butte - an isolated hill or mountain, usually with a flat top

buttress - an external prop or a support added to steady a structure

camouflage - a disguise or deception used by nature to protect animals

capital - the uppermost portion of a column that supports a roof

column - a rigid, slender, upright support for a building

complementary - completing; a necessary component of something

composition - the organization of parts of an artwork to make a unified whole

contour drawing - linear representation showing all of the parts of a subject

crayon resist - the result of applying a wet wash of ink or watercolor over a solid crayon line or shape

cupola - a small roof-top structure, often with a domed roof

dormer window - a window set in the sloping part of a roof

eaves - the overhanging lower edges of a roof

gesture drawing - a quick line recording of the outer edge of a figure or shape

horizon line - the line that forms the visual boundary between foreground and background

keystone - a wedge-shaped stone set in the center of an architectural arch to counterbalance the inward thrust

line quality - the thinness, thickness, smoothness, or irregularity of a line. It can be varied by tool or pressure.

lintel - a horizontal beam that supports weight above an opening such as a door or window

metamorphosis - a complete change of form, structure, or substance

modular - describing a design unit that is repeated

overlapping - a technique for showing depth by drawing one object behind another, showing only the part seen

pediment - a low shape, usually triangular, above a horizontal structure that provides an angle to the roof

perceptual - pertaining to the senses, particularly sight

perspective - the technique that represents volume and spacial relationships on a flat surface

positive/negative - figure and background; solid and open space

proportion - the relation of parts to the whole in a composition

radial symmetry - visual balance from the center outward

rhythm - a principle of art in which elements such as color, line, shape, and so on are repeated in a pattern

shape - a flat area enclosed by its boundary

space - the designed surface of a picture; the illusion of depth in a 2-D plane

spire - a tall, pointed, pyramidal structure on a roof; a steeple

tessellation - a shape that, when repeated, leaves no space between shapes. For example, square, oblong, or hexagonal floor tiles

texture - the visual (simulated) and/or tactile (actual) quality of a surface

topography - the study of the relief features of a surface

tower - a structure that is tall and narrow

transparency - a technique of drawing that shows all the details of a form in the background through the form in front of it

Name _____

School Months

	1	2	3	4	5	6	7	8	9
uses the elements of art									
applies the principles of art									
uses details									
shows proportions									
cuts neatly									
glues neatly									
shows craftsmanship									
completes drawings									
writes clearly									
uses and understands new terms									
takes risks									